"IN THEIR OWN WORDS"

THE ROMANS

Robert Hull

W
FRANKLIN WATTS
LONDON•SYDNEY

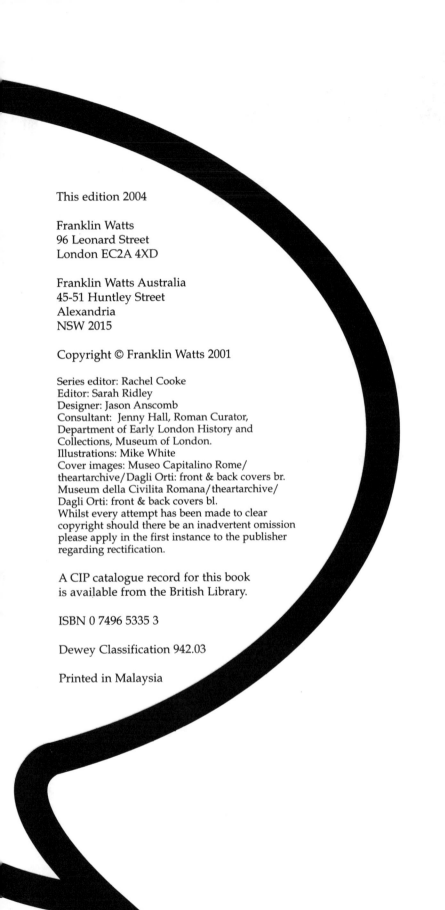

This edition 2004

Franklin Watts
96 Leonard Street
London EC2A 4XD

Franklin Watts Australia
45-51 Huntley Street
Alexandria
NSW 2015

Series editor: Rachel Cooke
Editor: Sarah Ridley
Designer: Jason Anscomb
Consultant: Jenny Hall, Roman Curator,
Department of Early London History and
Collections, Museum of London.
Illustrations: Mike White
Cover images: Museo Capitalino Rome/
theartarchive/Dagli Orti: front & back covers br.
Museum della Civilita Romana/theartarchive/
Dagli Orti: front & back covers bl.
Whilst every attempt has been made to clear
copyright should there be an inadvertent omission
please apply in the first instance to the publisher
regarding rectification.

A CIP catalogue record for this book
is available from the British Library.

ISBN 0 7496 5335 3

Dewey Classification 942.03

Printed in Malaysia

"IN THEIR OWN WORDS"

Introduction

The Roman People

Who were the Romans? At first, before 500BC, they were a small community of farmers living in the hills of central Italy. They spoke Latin, the language of Latium, the district where they lived. Needing security, this tough people made alliances[1] with other small communities, and took them over.

Over the course of two or three hundred years the Romans became the strongest people in Italy. In another hundred years or so, their power had spread like a fire into parts of North Africa, over to what is now Turkey and through central and northern Europe, up to Scotland and west to Spain.

As invaders, the Romans were ruthless. If the nation they were invading didn't co-operate, they could be terrifyingly cruel, as when they destroyed Carthage and Corinth in the same year. Once the local people had seen how ruthless the Romans could be, it wasn't difficult for the Roman army to keep the peace, even though there were rebellions, like that of Boudicca in Britain.

The Roman peace, maintained by the Roman army, brought great prosperity to large areas of Europe and Africa. The conquered people often learnt Latin and followed Roman lifestyles, building Roman-style buildings and cities. Local leaders became Roman generals and governors. Many local customs and beliefs were absorbed into the Roman lifestyle.

This huge empire was ruled from Rome where there were many murderous struggles for power. Initially, the Republic[2], as it was known, was governed by a body of rich men, the Senate[3], together with an Assembly. They made the laws and selected two Consuls[4] to impose them. Then, to stop all the power struggles, Augustus was declared Princeps[5], the leading citizen, and he ruled like a dictator or king. Augustus was also given the title Imperator – great general – and this came to be the title of all the rulers of Rome after that – emperor.

Rome grew and grew, with thousands of people flooding in from all corners of the empire. Many of them were

1. **alliance**: political agreement to help each other.

AVGVS

RESPVI

RESTI

2. **the Republic**: the period, c. late 6th century to 1st century BC, when Rome was ruled by two elected Consuls rather than a king or emperor.
3. **the Senate**: the group of rich Roman citizens (Senators) who advised the rulers of Rome. Its power was greatest during the Republic.
4. **the Consuls**: the two chief adminstrators (or magistrates) of the Roman Republic.
5. **Princeps**: the leading citizen of Rome.

'enslaved' – they'd become slaves through defeat in war, though there were fewer of these once the empire reached its limits. Emperors were anxious that this mass of people might become restless so they gave them holidays in abundance, entertainments, games, free food and even cash hand-outs.

It became increasingly difficult to recruit people for the army, so necessary for maintaining an empire of this size. Also, after 450 years of dominating huge areas of land, other groups of people like the Saxons and the Goths started attacking parts of the empire. In Britain, Emperor Hadrian pulled back Roman troops to the great wall he had built. Gradually the Romans were forced to leave parts of their empire altogether, withdrawing from France and Britain in the AD400s.

Roman Writings

6. **amphitheatre**: open-air buildings for theatre or other entertainment.
7. **baths**: public baths, rather than bathrooms.
8. **villa**: a large country house and farm.

After the decline of the Roman Empire, evidence of their presence remained in the previously conquered lands. Huge architectural structures like amphitheatres[6], baths[7], villas[8] and street layouts exist in some places to this day. Millions of artifacts such as coins, statues, pottery and even pieces of clothing survive to shed light on everyday life.

We also have written evidence from this time which has survived in different forms, depending on what part of the empire they come from. In Pompeii, Italy, volcanic ash from the eruption of Mount Vesuvius killed thousands of people in AD79. It preserved a wealth of material, from messages scratched on the walls (Roman graffiti) to dedications to the gods written on broken bits of pottery. One piece of graffiti read: 'Health to you, Lavinia, may you sneeze sweetly.'

Many messages were carved or inscribed on durable materials such as stone, metal and pottery. Monuments of all kinds were covered with inscriptions. These included the brief ones on gravestones and milestones to longer ones where a code of law, a farming calendar or a person's career were written down. Some of these have survived.

However, even where the writing was inscribed on a durable material, such as bronze, it hasn't always survived. The very earliest Roman writing we have is a law code dating from the 5th century BC. This was initially inscribed on bronze tablets known as 'The Twelve Tables' yet these tablets have not survived. We know of them because writers at the time have included the contents of these laws in their own writings.

Romans used papyrus for their 'books', creating paper from dried strips of this reed that became rolls of paper. Generally, papyrus perishes easily but in Egypt, where the climate is very hot and dry, some of these books have survived, buried in the remains of buildings.

Sometimes we can read the writings of the Romans because they have been preserved by medieval monks. They were responsible for copying large numbers of volumes, so that many of the Latin texts of the papyrus rolls survive, even if the roll itself has perished.

In everyday life, Romans often used wooden tablets to write short messages, lists or notes. These slats of wood might be written on using ink and a pen, or by a stylus that scratched the words into a thin layer of wax. Later the tablet could be reused by smoothing over the wax. In Britain, a number of these wooden tablets have survived buried in wet or damp conditions where the air cannot start the rotting process.

All these writings – the tablets, the graffiti, the hundreds of books, the 100,000 or so carved Latin inscriptions, as well as many in Greek – are the voices of Roman people who lived around 2,000 years ago. 'That's all I have to say,' ends one gravestone inscription. We can also hear them speak through the surviving books about history, geography and natural history; the poetry, plays, letters and speeches for the law-courts. We hear how the poet Juvenal hated Rome and how the governor Pliny wasn't sure how to run his local jail. Often a point of view is being expressed so we have to think who wrote these words, and why. All the quotes selected in this book have been translated from Latin or Greek and translations vary.

1. **orator**: a public speaker.

2. **Senator**: member of the Senate. See page 4.
3. **Troy**: an ancient city located in modern Turkey. In myth, it was destroyed by the Greeks, who entered the city hidden inside the wooden horse – a gift to the Trojans (the people of Troy).

Biographies of the Main Contributors

Cato the Elder (234-149BC) was the first Roman writer to use Latin rather than Greek. He wrote about law and war. His books on the origins of Rome and agriculture survive.

Cicero (106-43BC) was one of Rome's greatest orators[1] and politicians, and a writer of many books, speeches and letters.

Martial (c. AD40-103/4) came from Spain but lived most of his life in Rome. He is one of the best Roman poets and over 1,500 of his poems survive.

Pliny the Elder (AD23-79) was a great scholar and admiral who wrote 102 books that have not survived, and a 37-volume work, *Natural History*, that survives.

Pliny the Younger (c. AD61-112), his nephew and adopted son, was also a writer and lawyer who eventually became the governor of Bithynia (modern Turkey) on the Black Sea.

Plutarch (c. AD46-127) was a Greek scholar and philosopher, who travelled through the eastern parts of the Roman Empire, lecturing for a while in Rome itself. He is famous for his biographies and writings on morals.

Seneca (c. 4BC-AD65) was from Cordoba in Spain, and was deputy governor of southern Spain for a while. He wrote tragic plays, philosophy, science and letters.

Strabo (c. 64BC-AD21), a Greek who settled in Rome in 29BC, wrote a *General History* that has not survived and a 17-volume book *Geography* that has.

Suetonius (born c. AD70), secretary to Emperor Hadrian, came from a well-off family. He wrote history in the form of biographies of famous people.

Tacitus (AD56-120), one of the great Roman historians, came from an aristocratic family and was a Senator[2]. He wrote the biography of his father-in-law, Agricola, Governor of Britain, as well as a history of Rome.

Virgil (70-19BC) was a poet. In his *Aeneid*, he told the story of Aeneas who escaped from the destruction of Troy[3] to come to Italy and found Rome. He wrote about life in the country also.

Rome and the Romans

Writers give us a vivid picture of Rome, the centre of the Roman Empire. They show us a great city on a river (the Tiber), the trading centre of the western world, where ocean-going ships line the waterfront. Here is a city teeming with people from all corners of Italy and the empire, full of impressive buildings – civic centres, libraries, temples and bridges. This Rome is praised for its practical achievements, especially its marvellous water-supply.

However, the Rome that the writers describe is also a dangerous, dirty city, full of noisy narrow alleys crammed with shops, trader's stalls and smoky workshops. Here most people live in crowded three-storey tenement[1] blocks that are sometimes tumble-down, and always a fire-risk.

1. **tenement**: a flat.

Early Rome

Titus Livius (Livy) came from northern Italy. He wrote a *History of Rome* in which he records the legend of how Rome was established. These writings may not be valuable as history but they show us how the Romans viewed their past.

When Troy[2] was captured, while Greeks took their revenge on the rest of the Trojans, two of them, Aeneas and Antenor, were spared ... because they had always argued for peace and the return of Helen[3]...

Aeneas came to Italy, to the land of King Latinus. *Latinus was told that the people were Trojans and their leader was the son of Anchises and the goddess Venus[4]; their city had been burnt down, and they had been driven from home, and were now looking for a place to live and found a city... Aeneas became a guest in the house of Latinus, who then added a family alliance to the political connection by giving his daughter in marriage to Aeneas. This event removed any doubt in the minds of the Trojans; their wanderings had come to an end, and they had found a permanent settled home.*

Livy, late 1st century BC

2. **Troy**: see page 7.
3. **Helen**: the Greek queen whose abduction by the Trojans started the war between them and the Greeks.
4. **Venus**: the Roman goddess of love.

Tacitus, an historian, wrote these words at the beginning of his *Annals of Rome*.

In the beginning, kings ruled the city of Rome.

Tacitus, c. AD100

In his *Compendium of Roman History* written in the 4th century, Eutropius records the legend of Romulus and Remus, orphaned baby boys who were brought up by a mother wolf and went on to establish Rome. He compiled his work from books by Livy and Tacitus long after the events he was recording.

The Roman Empire – and human memory can hardly think of any empire smaller to start with or one which grew so large – began with Romulus, who with his twin brother Remus was born to Rhea Silva, a Vestal Virgin[5], and [the legend says] of the god Mars[6]. At the age of 18, while he was still robbing shepherds, he founded a small town on the Palatine Hill, on 21 April, in the third year of the Sixth Olympiad, and the 394th year after the destruction of Troy.

Eutropius, c. AD370

Dionysius of Halicarnassus, a Greek teacher and historian, came to Rome in about 30BC. He included these stories of the building projects undertaken by the early king, Tarquinius Superbus (reigned 534-510BC), in his book, *Roman Antiquities*. He wrote about Rome 500 years before his own lifetime.

He [Tarquinius Superbus] chose from the people those who were loyal to him and employed them in military service. He compelled the rest to do forced labour on public projects, because he believed that when the poor people had no work to do kings like himself were vulnerable. He also wanted to finish the public works started by his grandfather. These included improving Rome's drainage system, where digging had actually begun, and adding a line of columns all the way round the race-track in the amphitheatre[7], where only

5. Vestal Virgin: one of the virgins who kept the fire alight at the temple of Vesta in Rome. Vesta was goddess of the hearth.

6. Mars: the Roman god of war.

7. amphitheatre: see page 5.

the foundations had been laid. He set the poor to work on all this, quarrying stone, cutting timber, escorting carts full of building materials, even carrying some of it on their backs – all in return for a miserable handout of grain.

Dionysius of Halicarnassus, c. 30BC

The Great City of Rome

Aelius Aristides, a Greek traveller and writer, made his first visit to Rome in AD144. His praise of the city became famous. *Whatever is grown or made anywhere in the world can be found here. So many merchant ships sail to you with their varied cargoes, all through the year, that it seems that you are truly the warehouse of the world. We can see ships with cargoes from India, and Arabia ... with clothing from Babylon, and luxuries from the lands beyond... Egypt, Sicily, and the civilised parts of Africa are your farms.*

Aelius Aristides, AD144

Buildings and Architecture

This 4th century AD document lists the main buildings and features of Rome.

Libraries	– 28
Bridges	– 8
Hills	– 7
Fields	– 8
Forums[1]	– 11
Basilicas[2]	– 10
Baths[3]	– 11
Aqueducts[4]	– 19
Roads	– 29

1. **forum**: a city square and market, often a popular meeting place.
2. **basilica**: a public hall used as a law court.
3. **baths**: see page 5.
4. **aqueduct**: a bridge built as a water channel.

It lists the houses and smaller buildings too, in one district.

5. tenements: See page 8.

Tenements[5]	*– 2,777*
Private houses	*– 140*
Storehouses	*– 25*
Baths	*– 63*
Fountains	*– 120*
Bakeries	*– 20*

The Regionaries, c. AD300-350

Pliny the Elder celebrated Rome's public supply of water in his 37-volume book, *Natural History*.

If we think of the plentiful supply of water to the people, for baths, and ponds, and canals, for household purposes, for gardens, for homes in the suburbs and country houses; and then if we think of the distances that water is brought from sources in the hills, and the arches that have been constructed, the mountains pierced through, the valleys levelled, we have to admit that there is nothing more amazing in the universe.

Pliny the Elder, c. AD50

Din, Bustle and Danger

One of the best Roman poets, Martial, wrote poetry of many kinds – much of it amusing, realistic pictures of Rome, like this description of its din and bustle.

Even before daybreak there are the bakers shouting, then all morning you can't hear yourself think for the schoolteachers' bawling and the thwack of the beatings they hand out. All day long you hear coppersmiths' hammers at it... The ting-ting-tinging of the goldsmith never stops for a second, nor does the jingling of money-changers' coins on their tables...

Martial, c. AD86

At times Rome's streets became impossibly cluttered. Martial congratulated Emperor Domitian on ordering shopkeepers to 'retreat' to their shops.

Pushy shopkeepers had taken over all Rome, and inside the boundaries of Rome no-one had the faintest idea where shop boundaries were. Lord Germanicus[1], you have instructed these shrunken streets to widen out again. Roads that had narrowed to alleyways are back to roads again. No longer do you find every stone pillar draped with a stack of wine-jars, making people walk round in the mud. You no longer nearly fall on a razor that's being sharpened in the middle of a crowd. You no longer find the width of the street taken over by drinkers from some foul pub. Suddenly, the barber, the pub-owner, the cook, the butcher and the rest, are all keeping their business inside their shop-limits. And – look! – here we have Rome again, where yesterday there was one great dirty shop.

Martial, c. AD86

1. **Germanicus**: a title granted to the Emperor Domitian in AD84.

Rome at night brought its dangers – and not just from thieves and robbers, said the poet Juvenal.

From high up near the rooftops a piece of pottery comes crack down on my head! It's the same every time – some old cracked jug or some damaged bits of goods being thrown out of the window – smash! on the pavement. You take your life in your hands at night every time you pass an open window. Only a fool would go out to dinner without making a will!

Juvenal, c. AD90

Leaders and Emperors

Rome was never a democracy ruled by an elected leader, or group of leaders. At the very beginning, before about 500BC, there were kings. Then, when it was called a Republic[2], it was governed by an Assembly and a body of Senators[3], with two Consuls[4], who ruled for a year. In times of upheaval or war, a single dictator might bully his way to the top.

Later, there were internal wars caused by arguing groups, until Julius Caesar became dictator, sole ruler, for life. After his murder came Augustus, who made himself Princeps[5] in 27BC. From then on Rome was ruled by emperors.

Other Romans had powerful jobs, including censors[6], generals and governors of the provinces[7] in the empire.

2. **Republic**: see page 4.
3. **Senators**: see page 7.
4. **Consuls**: see page 4.
5. **Princeps**: see page 4.
6. **censor**: a magistrate or administrator who assessed Roman citizens for taxation, voting rights, military service and public morals.
7. **province**: an administrative region of the Roman Empire.

Sulla

Appian, a Greek lawyer from Alexandria, wrote a military history of Rome. In it he described how Sulla made himself dictator by leading an army to Rome in about 80BC.

Sulla pronounced sentence of death on 40 Senators and about 1600 knights. He seems to have been the first to write public lists of those he wanted to be punished, and to reward murderers and informers, and punish people found hiding his victims. Soon he added other Senators to the list. Some were caught unawares and killed where they were found, at home, in the street, in a temple. Others were taken and heaved through the city and thrown at Sulla's feet. Others were dragged through the streets and kicked to death, the spectators being too frightened to utter a word of protest. Some were expelled from Rome and had their houses and possessions confiscated. There were spies everywhere, looking for people fleeing the city, and killing anyone they captured.

Appian, c. AD130-140

Julius Caesar

Suetonius' book, *Lives of the Twelve Caesars*, is crammed with fact and scandal. His book about Julius Caesar (100-44BC) described how he was captured by pirates.

Winter had already set in when he sailed for Rhodes and was captured by pirates. They kept him prisoner for nearly forty days, to his great annoyance. He only had a doctor and two valets[1] with him, having sent the rest of his staff away to borrow the ransom money. As soon as the fifty talents[2] arrived and the pirates put him ashore, he raised a fleet and went after them. He had often smilingly sworn, while still in their power, to capture them and crucify[3] them. And that is just what he then did... Caesar was not naturally vindictive; and if he crucified the pirates who held him to ransom, this was only because he had sworn in their presence that he would do so. And he first mercifully cut their throats.

Suetonius, c. AD100

1. **valet**: a personal servant.
2. **talent**: an ancient unit of money in Rome equal to 2,400 gold pieces
3. **crucify**: to put to death on a cross.

Suetonius described the murder of Julius Caesar in 44BC.

It was about ten o'clock when he set off for the Senate[4]... As he went, someone handed him a note revealing the details of the plot against him, but he only added it to the bundle of petitions and papers in his left hand, which he intended to read later. Several sacrifices were made, and then, though the sacrifice omens[5] were not good, Caesar entered the Senate, saying Spurinna prophesied wrongly. "The Ides[6] of March are here," he said. "They have come," said Spurinna, "but they have not gone." As soon as Caesar took his seat the conspirators crowded round him, pretending to pay him their respects. Tillius Cimber ... came up close, pretending to ask a question. Caesar was waving him away, but Cimber gripped Caesar's shoulder. "What's this? Violence!" Caesar cried, and at that moment one of the Casca brothers slipped behind Caesar and

4. **Senate**: see page 4.

5. **omen**: a sign of some future event.
6. **Ides**: in the Roman calander, the 15th day of the months of March, May, July, October and the 13th day of the other months.

stabbed him just below the throat. Caesar grasped Casca's arm and ran it through with his stylus; he was struggling free when another dagger caught him in the breast. Confronted by a ring of drawn daggers, he drew the top of his gown over his face... Twenty-three dagger-thrusts went home as he stood there. Caesar had not uttered a sound once Casca's blow had drawn a groan from him; though some say that when he saw Marcus Brutus was about to deliver the second blow, he reproached him in Greek with: "You too, my son?"

Suetonius, c. AD100

Augustus Wins Power

Tacitus related how Augustus had himself made Princeps[7] in 27BC.

Augustus won over the soldiers with cash gifts, the common people with cheap grain, and everyone in general with the benefits of tranquillity. In the meantime he himself managed to take over the powers of the Senate, the magistrates[8], and the laws.

Tacitus, c. AD100

Caligula

Caligula (ruled AD37-41) was assassinated after four years as emperor. Suetonius described him.

He was very tall, with an enormous body on spindly legs... Though he had a hairy body he was bald on top. He made it a crime – punishable by death – to look down on him from above as he passed... He had galleys[9] built that had ten banks of oars, with their poops[10] crusted with jewels, and sails of many colours. On board there were large baths, colonnades and banqueting halls – not to mention various kinds of vine and even apple-trees, growing of course. He used to take early morning cruises along the coast in these boats, sprawled on his couch, listening to songs and choruses.

Suetonius, c. AD100

7. **Princeps**: see page 4.
8. **magistrate**: a public officer who administrated Roman law.
9. **galley**: a boat.
10. **poop**: a high deck at the back of a boat.

Trajan

Pliny the Younger became Governor of Bithynia[1]. His correspondence with Emperor Trajan (ruled AD97-117) is a fascinating picture of the top levels of Roman government.

I pray you, sir, to give me advice on the following matter. I am not sure whether I ought to carry on using the public slaves in various towns as prison-warders, as previously, or to put soldiers on guard-duty in the prisons. I fear that the slaves are not reliable enough, but on the other hand the duties would take up the time of a good number of soldiers. For the time being I have put soldiers on duty beside the slaves, as warders ... but I can see this might lead to a neglect of duty on both sides, when each could blame the other.

Pliny the Younger, between AD111 and 113

Trajan's reply

There is no need, my dear Pliny, for more soldiers to be transferred to guard-duty in the prisons. We should carry on with the custom of the province[2] and use public slaves... And as you say, if we mix soldiers with public slaves, the chief danger is that both sides will become careless. Let us keep to the general rule that as few soldiers as possible should be called away from active service.

Trajan, between AD111 and 113

1. **Bithynia**: now northern Turkey.

2. **province**: see page 13.

ATVSPOPVLVSQVEROMAN

CAESARI DIVI NERVAE F NER

ANO AVG GERM DACICO PO

MOTRIB POT XVII IMP VI COS

CLARANDVMO VANTAE ALTITV

Peoples of the Empire

Rome became the ruler of many peoples, with a mostly peaceful empire stretching from Syria to Scotland. Gradually the people of these lands became 'Romanized', living a Roman-style life in Roman-style towns, and whose leaders might become Roman citizens.

But the path to that civilized peace was blood-soaked. Roman cruelty destroyed cities and murdered and enslaved thousands of people. Roman ruthlessness was what built an empire, even though Roman common sense lured defeated peoples into becoming good Romans.

Roman Britain

The Romans first invaded Britain in 55BC under Julius Caesar but, having set up trade links, soon left, only to return in force in AD43. This time they stayed for nearly four hundred years, leaving a permanent stamp on the country.

Julius Caesar wrote his *Commentaries* as a record of his great achievement in the Gallic Wars, which included the conquest of Gaul[2] and his invasion of Britain. The books mostly concern themselves with the military campaign but he did also give a description of southern Britain:

The interior of Britain is inhabited by people who claim on the strength of their own tradition to be indigenous to the island; the coastal districts by immigrants from Belgic territory who came after plunder and to make war – nearly all of them are called after the tribes from which they originated. Following their invasion they settled down there and began to till the fields. The population is very large, their homesteads thick on the ground and very much like those in Gaul, and the cattle numerous. As money they use either bronze or gold coins or iron bars with a fixed standard of weight. Tin is found inland, iron on the coast, but in small quantities; the bronze they use is imported. There is every type of timber as in Gaul, with the exception of beech and pine. They have a taboo against eating hare, chicken,

2. **Gaul**: roughly modern France, inhabited by the Gauls, a Celtic people.

and goose, but they rear them for amusement and pleasure. The climate is more temperate than in Gaul, the cold spells being less severe.

Julius Caesar, 50BC

Strabo described the British and their way of life in his 17-volume book, *Geography*. He died in AD21, so his information probably came from Caesar's descriptions of his campaigns against the Britons.

1. **Gauls**: see page 17.

Their way of life is a bit like the Gauls'[1] but much cruder and more barbaric. For example, though they have plenty of milk, some of them do not know how to make cheese, nor do they know anything about how to keep gardens or farms. In wars they mostly use chariots, like the Gauls. Their cities are the forests. They cut down the trees and fence in a large round space. In this enclosure they build their huts and corral their cattle, but they do not stay in any one place for long.

Strabo, late 1st century BC

The Romans invaded again in AD43 and began the process of making Britain a province[2] of the empire. Tacitus explained why a Roman colony was founded at Colchester in AD49.

2. **province**: see page 13.
3. **Iceni**: a Celtic tribe who held land in East Anglia.

Its mission was to protect the country against revolt and familiarize the provincials with law-abiding government.

Tacitus, c. AD100

Not everyone was happy. Suetonius described how the Romans treated Boudica, the widow of the King of the Iceni[3], which led to her famous rebellion, in AD60.

Prasutagus, King of the Iceni, after a long prosperous life, arranged for the Roman Emperor to be his heir, alongside the king's two daughters. He hoped by this tactic to keep his kingdom and household free from Roman attack. But he could not, as it turned out. His kingdom and household were plundered by Roman officers and slaves as if they were prizes in war. At the start of this, the king's widow, Boudica, was beaten and her daughters were raped. The Icenian chiefs had their family estates taken from them, as if the Romans had been given every scrap of the land. The king's relatives were treated like slaves.

Suetonius, c. AD100

Suetonius went on to relate the events in the rebellion itself: the British burnt London, Colchester and St Albans and 70,000 people died. Then the Romans returned to the fight. *In wedge formation, they thrust forward. The cavalry, lances extended, demolished all remaining resistance. The Britons who were left had difficulty escaping because their ring of wagons blocked the exits. It was a great victory. According to one report nearly 80,000 Britons died. Our own casualties numbered about 400 dead and a slightly larger number of wounded. Boudica poisoned herself.*

Suetonius, c. AD100

Tacitus described how the Romans dealt with the Celtic enemy on the island of Mona (now Anglesey) in AD61. *The enemy lined the shore in a dense armed mass. Among them were black-robed women with dishevelled hair like furies, brandishing torches. Close by stood Druids[4], raising their hands to heaven and screaming dreadful cries… The groves[5] devoted to Mona's barbarous superstitions he [Seutonius Paulinus, the Roman commander] demolished. For it was their religion to drench their altars in the blood of prisoners and consult their gods by means of human entrails.*

Tacitus, c. AD100

4. **Druids**: religious leaders of the Celts. 5. **grove**: a small group of trees. The Druids performed many of their religious rituals in sacred groves.

Agricola was Governor of Britain from AD78 to 85. As well as campaigning in Scotland, he worked carefully at 'Romanizing' the British. Tacitus praises his work in

civilizing the Britons in his histories – though we need to remember he was Agricola's son-in-law.

Agricola had to deal with people who were ignorant and liked fighting; so he aimed to get them used to a life of peace and harmony... He helped them build temples, public squares and fine houses... He educated the sons of the native chiefs, and said he preferred British ability to the trained skills of the Gauls[1]. The result was that instead of loathing our foreign Latin language they tried to speak it effectively. Our national dress appealed to them as well, and togas began to appear everywhere. The British thought of their new Roman buildings, baths[2] and banquets as signs of their 'civilization'. But really they were marks of enslavement.

Tacitus, c. AD100

Tacitus also gave to Calgacus, a Scottish chief, words which show the Romans in a self-deceiving light.

"They rob, plunder and kill and call that 'empire'. They create a desolate waste land, and call that 'peace'."

Tacitus, c. AD100

Violent Conquest

The Romans were brutal in their quashing of the revolt that began in East Anglia. Other acts of violence in the empire have been recorded. Rome fought three long wars against Carthage in North Africa, from 264 to 146BC. The chapters which the historian Cassius Dio wrote about them have been lost. However, his words about the end of Carthage in 146BC were summarized by Zonaras, who must have read the book before its loss.

When Scipio took Carthage he sent this message to the Senate[3]: "Carthage is captured. What are my orders now?"... As a result of discussion all the Senate were unanimously in favour of destroying Carthage, because they

1. **Gauls**: see page 17.
2. **baths**: see page 5.
3. **Senate**: see page 4.

*were sure its people would not keep the peace permanently.
So the whole city was destroyed and blotted from existence.*

Cassius Dio, c. AD200; Zonaras 11th century AD

In his book, *A Description of Greece*, published in AD174,
Pausanias described the total destruction of Corinth by the
Romans in 146BC.

*On the third day after the battle Mummius proceeded to
storm Corinth and set it on fire. Most of those found in the
city were killed, but the women and children were sold into
slavery... Mummius demolished the walls of all the cities
that made war against the Romans.*

Pausanias, c. AD150

4. province: see
page 13.

Roman Order

Once a land had been invaded and settled, the Romans were
talented in bringing peace and prosperity to the province[4]. In
his speech of praise to Rome in AD144, Aelius Aristides
celebrated Roman order.

*The empire is immense and its territories widely spread, but
it is not so much the boundaries themselves that make it a
great empire – it is the perfect policing of its territories...
You could compare it with a strongly-fenced and well-swept
front yard.*

Aelius Aristides, AD144

Many Greeks, like the writer Plutarch, were grateful to
Rome, up to a point, for bringing peace and order.

*The greatest blessings that cities can enjoy are peace, and
prosperity. As far as peace is concerned there is now no need
even to strive for it, because we have it. All war – both here in
Greece and outside it – has been banished; it has disappeared.
As for freedom, people have as much as their rulers give to
them, and perhaps more would not be a good thing.*

Plutarch, c. AD100

21

Citizenship

Men from all corners of the empire might be made Roman citizens, with rights to vote and even be elected to the Senate. Many Romans feared this idea. Claudius, emperor from AD41 to AD54, did not. He wanted 'excellence from everywhere'. Suetonius related – or partly invented – a typical speech objecting to more citizens to which Claudius then replies.

Aren't there enough non-Romans in the Senate already, peoples such as Venetians and the Insubrian Gauls[1], without bringing in more hordes of foreigners, like gangs of prisoners? Soon there'll be no career left for the aristocrats who are left, or for the less well-off Senators[2] of Latium... Every post will be filled by rich men whose grandfathers and great-grandfathers commanded enemy tribes in battles against Roman armies... Are we supposed to forget that Roman men were killed right next to the Capitoline Castle here in Rome by the ancestors of these very same Gaulish people? Let them become Roman citizens, by all means. But never, never should they wear – and cheapen – the glorious insignia of the Senate[2].

Suetonius, c. AD100

1. **Gaul**: see page 17.
2. **Senator & Senate**: see page 7 and 4.
3. **Sabine**: one of an ancient people of Italy from a region north-east of Rome.

These ideas and speeches did not impress Emperor Claudius. He argued against them, and made this speech in the Senate:

I think of the experience of my own family, not least that of its founder, Clausus, who was a Sabine[3], and who was made a Roman citizen and a Senator at the same time. It inspires me to follow the same policy, and bring excellence to Rome from everywhere.

Suetonius, c. AD100

MAXIMOT

Soldiers and the Army

In Rome's early days its army was not full-time. Then the first emperor, Augustus, decided that a soldier should serve for 16 years, followed by four years as a 'veteran'. Later it became 20 years, plus another five as a veteran. Legionary soldiers were Roman citizens but in times of need, any man between the ages of 17 and 46 could be called up, including slaves occasionally, as in the Punic Wars against Carthage.

There were soldiers for the defence of Rome, and soldiers defending the boundaries of the empire. The army was divided into legions of 5-6,000 men, backed up by non-citizen auxilliary units. Four legions[4] defended Britain. In peacetime, the governor of the province[5] was in charge of the army. The generals came from the ruling classes and served in the government service for career advancement.

4. **legion:** a unit of the Roman army.
5. **province:** see page 13.

Ruthless Roman armies built the Roman Empire, then defended the Roman peace, leaving stone inscriptions wherever they went.

Roman Readiness and Discipline

The Roman military emphasis was on physical fitness, training exercises, daily marching and techniques like camp-building. Their readiness, sheer numbers and war-machines made them very successful. Vegetius was a civilian who wrote about military affairs towards the end of the period of the empire; he summed up Roman attitudes in one sentence. **Whoever wants peace should be ready for war.**

Vegetius, c. AD390

Vegetius showed that the army was very tough.
Young soldiers must be given frequent practice on carrying loads of up to 60 pounds[6] marching along at a military pace... In the summer months a march of 20 Roman miles[7] must be completed in five hours.

Vegetius, c. AD390

6. **60 pounds:** approximately 28 kilograms.
7. **20 miles:** approximately 60 kilometres.

Josephus, a Jewish historian from Jerusalem, was born in AD37. He thought Roman success was due to training and discipline.

They do not wait for war to begin ... or sit around idle in peacetime, going into action only in emergencies. It's as if they were born primed for the battle, already armed. They never have a cease-fire in the middle of their training, and they do not wait for war to be declared. Their battle drills are the same as the real thing, and every man works hard at his daily training just as if he was on active service fighting. That's why they stand up to the strain of battle so well. There's no indiscipline to dislodge them out of their regular formation, no panic to incapacitate them, no work that will tire them out. You could say that their military exercises are bloodless battles, and their battles are bloody exercises.

He described the discipline of soldiers leaving their camp.

The trumpet sounds and every man springs to his post. On that signal the huts are dismantled and preparations made for departure. The trumpet then sounds, "Stand by to march!" At once they load the mules and wagons with the baggage and take their places like runners lined up and waiting for the starter's signal. Then they set fire to the camp, which if need be can be rebuilt just as efficiently and easily.

Josephus, c. AD80

Recruiting

The army should not accept just any recruits, according to Vegetius.

We need to ask ourselves from what trades we should select recruits, and from which we should absolutely reject them. Fishermen, fowlers[1], confectioners, weavers and in fact all those who appear to have been engaged in work that's suitable for the women's quarters, should not, in my opinion, be allowed anywhere near the barracks. On the other hand,

1. **fowler:** someone who hunts wild-fowl (game birds).

blacksmiths, metal-workers, wagon-makers, butchers and huntsmen – whether of stag or boar – are fitted for the services... And a number of military positions require men of good education. Examiners of recruits should take into account skill in writing and experience in arithmetic and book-keeping.

Vegetius c. AD390

Military Techniques and Skill

The army was skilled in bridge-building and other techniques that made invasion after invasion a smooth and successful operation. Strabo gave a clear description of how soldiers bridge rivers.

The boats to be used are flat-bottomed. They are anchored a short way upstream of where the bridge is to be. When the signal is given, soldiers in one boat let it drift down stream close to the bank, and when it is opposite the right place they throw into the river a wicker basket filled with stones and fastened by a rope. This acts as anchor for the boat. With the boat in position by the bank, the soldiers use the planks and clamps they have on board to make a gangway to the landing-place. Then they do the same with another boat, then another, until they reach the opposite bank.

Strabo, late 1st century BC

When Emperor Hadrian reviewed his troops on the Danube in AD121, the soldiers showed him what they could do. An inscribed stone described one soldier's feats.

Hadrian is my judge that I was able to swim across the waters of the great Danube in full battle-gear. When an arrow I shot high in the air was still hanging there, beginning to fall to earth, I fired another, hit the first and split it in two. No Roman or barbarian[2] ever got the better of me, not one soldier with his javelin or one archer with his bow. Here I lie, with my feats of arms recorded on stone

2. barbarian: anyone who was not a Roman.

25

that never forgets. It remains to be seen whether anyone else will do what I have done. But I was the first to have performed such feats.

Inscription, AD121

Everyday Army Life in England

Roman soldiers invaded, and defended Britain from AD43. In AD122, Emperor Hadrian ordered a wall to be built across the northern frontier of the Roman Empire (at that time, northern England). Since 1973, a number of wooden writing tablets have been found at Vindolanda, a fortlet just south of Hadrian's Wall. They date from the second century AD and give fascinating details of a soldier's life at that time.

One tablet listed a delivery of various wood items.

From Metto to Advectus, many greetings. Here is a list of the materials of wood I have sent to you with Saco:
34 wheel hubs
38 axles for carts
1 axle turned on a lathe
300 spokes
26 bed-planks
8 seats
2 knots
20 boards
6 benches
6 goat-skins

I trust you are in good health, brother.

Vindolanda tablet, 2nd century AD

One 'tablet' is a letter that arrived with a parcel from home.
I have sent you pairs of socks from Sattua, two pairs of sandals and two pairs of underpants.

Vindolanda tablet, 2nd century AD

One is evidently a bill for clothes, hairdressing and a saddle.

Cloaks – 6	11-and-a-half denarii[1] each, total 69 denarii
Headbands – 5	1 quarter of a denarius each, total 3 and three quarter denarii
Hair – 9 pounds[2] in weight	5-and-3 quarters denarii per lb, total 54-and-a-half denarii
Drawers – 10	2-and-a-half denarii each, total 25 denarii
Saddle – 1	12 denarii

Vindolanda tablet, 2nd century AD

1. **denarius** (plural **denarii**): Roman silver coin.
2. **pound**: approximately 0.5 kilograms.

Another seems like a list of food and drink in the store.

barley
Celtic beer
wine
sour wine
fish-sauce
pork-fat
spices
roe-deer
salt
young pig
ham
wheat
venison
honey beans
oysters

Vindolanda tablet, 2nd century AD

Family Life

Writers usually give us views of wealthy marriages and family life. Here, especially in the early days of the Roman Empire, the father's role as head of the family was like that of a dictator, a priest and a judge rolled into one. When a baby was born, the father would lift it in his arms to show he accepted it. The mother's role was to run the household, bring up the children and deal with the household accounts.

Wealthy families would employ a nurse to look after young children. When they were ready for education, the father would teach them himself, or, later in the era, they would be sent to school. School was an open space or rented area where they would learn arithmetic, reading and writing at first and then poetry, history, Greek and athletics.

Head of the Family

Cicero wrote many books, including one about old age where he describes the role of the male head of the household, the 'paterfamilias', who in early Rome had great power. One example he gave was Claudius, an elderly, blind paterfamilias, still firmly in charge.

He kept four vigorous sons in order, not to mention five daughters, a great household, and numerous workers and slaves. Instead of letting his mind grow slack and slow he kept it as flexible and lively as it had been in his youth. He didn't just direct his household, he ruled it. His slaves were scared of him; his children loved and admired him; everyone was fond of him. Under his roof there was discipline and deep respect for the old ways.

Cicero, c. 45BC

Marriages

The husband held the power in Roman marriages, but this didn't stop love from occuring. This imperial slave placed a moving inscription on his wife's grave.

She was the saint of my home, my life and my hope. Her wishes were the same as mine; so were her dislikes. None of

her thoughts was a secret from me. She was a busy spinner, careful with money, but generous to me. She took pleasure in taking meals only with me. She gave me good advice, she was wise and noble.

Tomb inscription, date unknown

In early Roman times, when marriages did not work, Roman husbands could divorce their wives for trivial reasons, or worse still, punish their wives, as related by Cato the Elder.

If you find that your wife is making love to someone else, you are allowed by law to put her to death without trial; but if you do the same thing yourself, she has no legal right to touch you.

Cato the Elder, c. 160BC

By the 3rd century AD, all Roman soldiers were allowed to marry. A Latin inscription at South Shields in Northumberland, erected by a Roman soldier from Syria, lamented the death of his young wife, a freed-woman[1] from the south of England.

To the spirits of the dead – and to Regina, his freed-woman and his wife, aged thirty, a woman of the Catuvellaunian people – Barates from Palmyra set up this tombstone.

Barates added a few words in his Syrian script.

Regina, the freed-woman of Barates – alas for her!

Tomb inscription, c. 3rd century AD

1. **freed-woman**: an ex-slave.

Children

Writers often tell us of the affection felt by Roman parents for their children. This verse by the poet Martial was written to be inscribed on a gravestone.

Here rests Erotion, her spirit faded from us, called away by Fate in her sixth winter. Whoever you are who has this little farm after me, make yearly sacrifice to her tiny soul; if you do, ... may your Lar[1] last forever, and your household be happy.

Martial, c. AD86

1. **Lar**: one of the Roman household gods who looked after the movement across the boundaries of the house.

This undated inscription on a tombstone at York was for the 13-year-old Corellia, daughter of Quitus Fortis.

Mysterious spirits of the dead ... towards whom the body's shadowy ghost hurries after the brief blaze of living, this is a father's lament for the death of an innocent daughter, whose cruelly unfair hopes of a life make her a victim to be pitied.

Tomb inscription, c. AD100

Such affection for deceased children contrasts with the practice of exposure. A Roman father had the right to reject a newborn baby, which would mean that it would be left to die in the open air.

This came from a letter written by a soldier to his young wife.

If you give birth – and the best of my good wishes to you for that – then, if the child is a boy, keep it; but if it is a girl, expose it. You told Aphrodisias to tell me, "Don't forget me." How could I forget you? I beg you not to worry. Year 29 of Caesar.

Letter, 1st century BC

In the 5th century BC Roman laws were inscribed on bronze plaques and exhibited in the Forum[2] at Rome. They tell us a lot about Roman customs and ways of life. One law ordered the exposure of 'deformed' babies. A hundred years later, baby-killing was outlawed.

Quickly kill ... a dreadfully deformed child.

Roman Law, 449BC

2. **Forum**: see page 10. In this case, the most important square in Rome.

Education at Home

The historian Plutarch, in his book *On the Education of Children*, written towards the end of the 1st century AD, tells us how Cato the Elder, like many Romans, preferred to educate his children himself. Plutarch also told us much about the kind of education children were given.

When his son was capable of learning, Cato himself took responsibility and taught him to read and write – even though he had a specialist slave called Chillon who was a teacher himself, with many pupils of his own. Cato said he didn't think it was right for his son to be disciplined by a slave, having his ears pulled for being late for lessons, or to be in debt to a slave for his son's education. So Cato himself taught him reading and writing, the law, and athletics. He taught him how to throw a spear, and fight in armour, and ride a horse and box. He taught him how to put up with heat and cold, and to swim through whirlpools and rapids. He says he wrote his book Histories in his own handwriting, and in large letters, especially so that his son could learn about the laws and customs of Rome.

Plutarch, c. AD100

Schools and Teachers

By the time of Cato it became normal to send your children to a teacher for education. The poet Horace was grateful for the trouble his father took to have him educated in Rome, in the style of the best families. This came from an autobiographical poem he wrote.

3. **Ides**: see page 14.
4. **Senator**: see page 7.

He was only a poor man with only a few acres, but he wouldn't send me to Flavius' school – where the important boys, sons of sergeant-majors, went, satchel and slate swinging from the left arm, clutching their fee on the Ides[3] of every month. Instead he bravely took me to Rome, to be taught the things every knight and Senator[4] wanted his own children taught. Anyone who noticed my clothes and the servants in attendance would have thought that the money for these items came from the family coffers. My father was the most trustworthy guardian imaginable, and accompanied me to all my classes.

Horace, c. 30BC

A native of Spain, Quintilian was a practising teacher and orator[1]. In a book on education, he said that children's learning should be interesting – an 'amusement'.

1. **orator**: see page 7.

Above everything else we need to make sure that the child, who is not yet old enough to love his studies, does not come to hate them... His learning must be made into a form of amusement. He must be questioned and praised and encouraged to be pleased with himself when he has done well... He should be allowed to believe that he has been successful more often than not, and stimulated to do his best by the kind of rewards that will appeal to him at his tender age.

Quintilian, c. AD70

Children were frequently beaten at school, for poor work or poor attention, so many Romans would have been shocked by what Quintilian said.

I disapprove of beating – though it is a regular custom... It is a disgraceful kind of punishment and only fit for slaves – an insult, as you'll realise if you imagine being beaten when you are few years old. Second, if tellings off and reprimands don't work, beating will only make things worse; the boy will just get used to it.

Modern children will approve of his views on holidays.

Boys restored and refreshed by a holiday will bring greater energy to their work.

Quintilian, c. AD70

The Woman's Role

Women ran the home, supervising the weaving, cooking and cleaning and looking after the children. This is a budget of household expenditure for January and February, AD1.

2. **drachma**: a unit of Greek currency, still in use during the Roman Empire in the Greek provinces.
1 drachma = 6 obol.

January-February	Drachmas[2]	Obol
Cloak	10	
Turnips for preserving	1	2
Hire of copper vessel for dyeing		2
Salt		2
Entertaining guest for one meal		4
Myrrh for burial of Phena's daughter		4
Wax and stylus for children		1
Pure bread		1/2
Lunch and beer for the weaver		3
Leeks for weaver's lunch		1
A pigeon		1
Grinding wheat for flour	1	2
Asparagus for dinner at fuller's feast		–
Cabbage for boy's dinner		1/2
Milk for the children		1/2
Birthday garlands		2
Pomegranates for the children	1	
Toys for the children		–

Household budget, c. AD1

3. **Ides**: see page 14.

Wealthy Roman women had a social life.

Claudia Severa to her Lepidina greetings.
On the 3rd day before the Ides[3] of September, sister, for the day of the celebration of my birthday, I give you a warm invitation to make sure that you come to us, to make the day more enjoyable for me by your arrival, if you come.
Give my greetings to your Cerialis. My Aelius and my little son send you their greetings.

Vindolanda tablet, 2nd century AD

Slaves

Roman life depended on slaves. Large numbers worked in private households; when the owner had a bath, or went shopping, he would have two or three slaves with him. They worked on farms and country estates. Pliny the Elder had at least 500 slaves, including some for his library; emperors made do with about 20,000. There were public slaves, often with the worst kind of work to do, like carrying water or clearing refuse, or labouring in the mines. The most expensive slaves were educated architects, musicians, literature and grammar teachers. Some became rich, making money in business, and were able to buy their freedom.

As time went on, slavery began to seem 'against natural law'. Most civilised and educated Romans treated their slaves more kindly. The laws improved; for instance it became illegal to sell a slave to be used as a gladiator. Emperor Hadrian deprived owners of the right to kill an offending slave.

Slaves as Objects

Many slaves were born into slavery, as the children of slaves. Thousands became enslaved as captives from wars, or by being kidnapped by pirates. Slaves were bought and sold at shops, auctions and markets like any traded goods. The owner kept his receipt, like this proof of ownership on papyrus from Egypt:

C Fabullius Macer, non-commissioned officer of the praetorian fleet of Misenum, in the ship called Tigris, has bought the slave called Abbas or Eutyches, a Mesopotamian[1] by nationality, who comes from beyond the Two Rivers. He is about seven years old. His price is two hundred denarii[2], plus poll tax[3] for importing him. Sold by Q Julius Pristus, ordinary seaman of the same fleet, in the same ship.

Papyrus document, AD166

1. **Mesopotamia:** modern Iraq.
2. **denarii:** see page 27.
3. **poll tax:** a tax per head (i.e. per person).

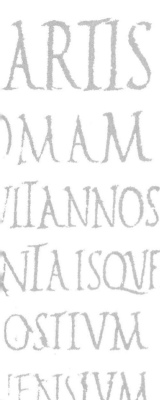

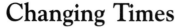

Changing Times

Varro, in his book *On Landed Estates*, seemed to treat the slaves in a more humane way.

Foremen should not be allowed to control their men with whips instead of words.

Avoid having too many slaves from one nation, for this is often a source of domestic quarrels. The foremen should be made more hard-working by being given rewards. That could include being given 'wives' from amongst their fellow slaves, to have children, so that they will be more reliable and attached to the place.

Varro, c. 80BC

Cicero believed in treating slaves kindly – they were 'fellow men'.

I'm glad to know ... that you live on good terms with your slaves. That fits in with your sensible outlook generally and your philosophy of life. "They're slaves," people say. Maybe, but still fellow men. "No, they're slaves." But they live under the same roof.

"They're still only slaves." No, friends – they are our humble friends... That's why I laugh at people who think it's beneath them to take their meals with their slaves. There's no reason for that, except the rude practice that's developed of surrounding the master at the dinner-table with a troop of slaves just standing there. While he wolfs down more than he can keep inside him, overloading a stomach till it forgets what it's actually for, his unlucky slaves can't move a muscle or say a word. Every whisper provokes the master's stick, and not even accidental noises – cough, sneeze, hiccough – are allowed – more stick. Any sound that breaks the silence results in pain. The slaves stand the whole night long, mute and famished.

Cicero, c. 45BC

Owners sometimes got rid of worn-out slaves. Suetonius described how Emperor Claudius tried to remedy this.

Claudius found out that a number of slaves who had either fallen ill or just become old and tired had been marooned by their owners on the island of Aesculepius in the middle of the River Tiber[1]. This was to avoid the trouble and expense of giving them medical attention. Claudius freed them, and said that none of them should return to their former owners; and that any owner who got rid of a sick slave should be charged with murder.

Suetonius, c. AD100

1. **River Tiber:** the river which flowed through Rome.

Cruelty

Slaves were often cruelly treated. Here is a story about Emperor Augustus as told by Suetonius.

He [Augustus] broke the legs of his secretary Thallus for having sold the contents of a personal letter for 500 denarii[2]. And he had the pedagogi[3] and servants of his son Gaius thrown into the river with heavy weights tied to their necks – because of the insolence and greed with which they had behaved out in the province[4] of Asia when Gaius was dying.

Seutonius, c. AD100

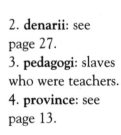

2. **denarii:** see page 27.
3. **pedagogi:** slaves who were teachers.
4. **province:** see page 13.

Apuleius, a writer from North Africa, described the condition of slaves working at a flour mill.

Their skin was black and blue with bruises, their backs covered with cuts from the whip. They were covered in rags, not clothes... They had been branded on the forehead and half their hair was shaved off. They wore iron chains on their legs.

Apuleius, c. AD160

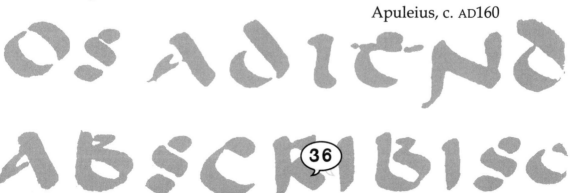

Rebellion and Escape

Well-treated slaves might be devoted to their masters but others tried to murder them or just escape. Escaped slaves who were caught were branded on the forehead. For worse offences they were killed, usually by crucifixion[4].

Given the poor treatment of many slaves, it is not surprising that there were slave rebellions. One occurred in Sicily in 100BC, as described by the historian Diodorus Siculus, who spent 30 years travelling and writing between 60-30BC.

There had never been a slave uprising to equal the one that now happened in Sicily... The whole island was on the point of falling into the hands of the runaways. Their aim was the complete destruction of their owners and masters. Most people were surprised by these upheavals, but to men of competent political judgement their occurrence did not seem surprising or unreasonable. The people exploiting this rich island had immense wealth, and practically all of these wealthy people were full of luxury, arrogance and insolence. So, the slaves' hatred of their masters increased at the same pace as did their masters' cruelty and insolence towards them. All the slaves' loathing for their masters erupted at the first opportunity and thousands of slaves gathered to destroy them.

Diodorus Siculus, c. 50BC

Slaves might try to escape. But they had to wear metal identity tags like this one, that could give them away. As they were made of metal, a few have survived the 2,000 years since they were made.

I am Asellus, slave of Praiectus, official on the staff of the prefect in charge of the grain-supply. I've escaped through the wall. Seize me, for I'm a fugitive, and return me to the barbers' quarter near the Temple of Flora[5].

Slave tag, date unknown

5. **Flora**: Roman goddess of spring and its flowering plants.

Working Life

In the Roman world, your livelihood depended greatly on your position in society. At the bottom came the slaves; men, women and children who did enormous amounts of domestic work inside the villas[1] of the well-off and farming work outside. Only poor people had no slaves. There were also public slaves, owned by the state who did all the nasty jobs like sweeping the streets.

1. **villa**: see page 5.

But there were also probably more than 150 specialist trades, every one with its own way of working. These craftsmen were workers or freed slaves. They were stone masons, carpenters, they carved ivory, they made pots and worked with leather. All of these goods were sold in shops by themselves, or by shopkeepers and traders.

The wealthy families earned their living from owning land and running large farm estates, or they worked as doctors, lawyers, politicians or high-ranking soldiers.

Trade and Respectability

In the Roman world, as recalled by Cicero, there were respectable ways of earning a living, and others that were to be avoided.

Now as far as trade and earning a living is concerned, there is work which is suitable for a gentleman, and work which is beneath him, and vulgar. The first of these are ways of earning a living which must be rejected as undesirable because they provoke ill-feeling in people – customs-collecting and money-lending for instance. Paid manual labour is also unworthy of a gentleman, and so is buying from wholesale merchants to re-sell immediately for profit... The least respectable occupations of all are those which cater to bodily pleasures: "Fishmongers, butchers, cooks, and poulterers, and fishermen," as the writer Terence says. And we can add to those: perfume-makers, and all kinds of dancer. But the professions which need intelligence, or which obviously benefit society – medicine, architecture,

teaching – are fine for those in that social position. Trade, if it is on a small scale, is a disreputable thing to be involved in. But if it is on a large scale, involving the import or export of large quantities of goods, then it is perfectly all right.

Cicero, c. 45BC

Wages

Some trades were paid better than others. Picture-makers earned six times as much a day as shepherds for instance, and teachers of public-speaking earned more than other teachers.

When wages and prices were rising quickly in AD296, Emperor Diocletian fixed a set of maximum wages. It makes it possible to compare the wages of professions.

2. **denarii**: see page 27.

Farm labourer, with maintenance – per day – 25 denarii[2]
Carpenter, with maintenance – per day – 50 denarii
Wall painter, with maintenance – per day – 75 denarii
Picture painter, with maintenance – per day – 150 denarii
Camel driver, with maintenance – per day – 25 denarii
Shepherd, with maintenance – per day – 20 denarii
Teacher of arithmetic, per boy – monthly – 75 denarii
Teacher of Greek and Latin Literature, per boy – monthly – 200 denarii
Teacher of rhetoric or public speaking, per boy – monthly – 250 denarii
Scribe, for the best writing, 100 lines – 25 denarii
Scribe, for second-quality writing, 100 lines – 20 denarii

The Edict on Maximum Prices, AD296

Trades

Most trades were not 'respectable'; not the thing that a gentleman, even a poor one, did for a living. But there were advantages as these workers often seemed to have plenty of free afternoons.

Workers making tiles stacked them in numbered rows, and sometimes scratched a remark on the end tile.

Amazingly, some of these tiles have survived.

At Dover one worker wrote on a tile:

I made 550 tiles.

To which another worker added on the same tile:

I smashed 51.

Tile, 1st or 2nd century AD

Another worker in London showed his disapproval of a workmates's behaviour.

Austalis has been wandering off on his own for the past 13 days.

Tile, 1st or 2nd century AD

Don't make bricks in summer, advised Vitruvius, who wrote a famous book on architecture and building.

Bricks must be made either in the spring or the autumn, so that they dry properly. Bricks made in mid-summer are liable to crack later. The sun is so strong that it very quickly bakes the outer skin dry, so the whole brick seems baked, while in fact the centre of the brick has still not dried out. Then as the inside dries it contracts, and cracks the already dried outer part... Bricks are best for use when they are about two years old; they will have dried out completely by then.

Vitruvius, c. AD1-10

Pliny the Elder explained how paper was made in Egypt.

Paper is manufactured from papyrus. The papyrus reed is split with a needle into strips that are very thin but as long as possible... All paper is 'woven' on a board dampened with water from the Nile, the muddy liquid acting as glue. First an upright layer is smeared on the table – the whole length of the papyrus is used and both its ends are trimmed. Then strips are laid across each other and make a complete criss-cross pattern, which is then squeezed in presses. The sheets are dried in the sun and then joined together.

Pliny the Elder, c. AD50

Barbers used iron razors and no soap. The poet Martial distrusted them, particularly one called Antiochus.

Anyone who doesn't want an early trip to the after-life should avoid Antiochus and his razor. The scars on my chin may look a bit like a boxer's, but they weren't the result of a scrap with a pugilist[1] – or my dear wife – no, they were left there by the skill, and the sharp metal, of the well-known barber Antiochius.

Martial, c. AD86

1. **pugilist**: a boxer.

Antiochus would have learned his trade by serving an apprenticeship[2] to a skilled barber. A papyrus from Oxyrhyncus in Egypt recorded an apprenticeship agreement.

This is an agreement between Platonis, also called Ophelia, daughter of Horion from the city of Oxyrhyncus, with her brother Plato as guardian, and Lucius, son of Ision and Tisasis, from Aphrodisium in the Small Oasis.
Platonis gives to Lucius her young slave Thermuthion as an apprentice to be trained for 4 years in the weaver's trade. Platonis herself will feed and clothe the girl, and bring Thermution to her master Lucius every day from sunrise to sunset to be taught everything related to the weaving trade. Her pay will be 8 drachmas a month for the first year, 12 for the second, 16 for the third and 20 for her last year as an apprentice. The girl will have 18 days off each year for festivals, but for each day that she is ill or does no work, she will work an extra day at the end of her time of service. Lucius, her weaving master, will pay the trade taxes and expenses.

Papyrus, 2nd century AD

2. **apprenticeship**: a period of training for a craft or trade, while working for the person teaching it.

3. **drachmas**: see page 33.

Farming

From their early days, in the 6th and 5th centuries BC, Romans were farmers. And they continued to be even when they had built a great empire. Farming was the basis of their prosperity. Owning and running a country farm was seen as an ideal way of life by many Roman writers.

The empire of the 1st century onwards needed huge amounts of wheat, much of it grown in Egypt and North Africa. If grain ran short people grew restless; it might mean trouble for the emperor. Free handouts of food were one answer. One of the reasons why the Romans wanted to add Britain to their empire was its rich farming land.

Laws and Rules for Farming

Some of the earliest Roman laws were about farming.

Any person who has deliberately cut down someone else's trees must pay 25 as[1] pieces for each tree.

Any adult person who deliberately pastures his cattle on someone else's crops, or cuts someone else's crops secretly at night, will be hanged and put to death as a sacrifice to Ceres[2].

Twelve Tables, 449BC

Calendars reminded farmers of important tasks.

Month of May. 31 days. The nones fall on the 7th day... The day has 14 and a half hours. The night has 9 and a half hours. The sun is in the sign of Taurus[3]. The month is under the protection of Apollo[4]. The grain fields are cleared of weeds. The sheep are shorn. The wool is washed. Young steers are put under the yoke. The vetch for fodder is cut. The lustration[5] of the grain fields is made. Sacrifices to Mercury[6] and Flora[7].

Source unknown, c. 2nd century BC

1. **as**: a copper coin.
2. **Ceres**: Roman goddess of agriculture.
3. **Taurus**: the constellation of the bull, one of the signs of the zodiac.
4. **Apollo**: Greek god of the sun, as well as healing, agriculture and animal husbandry. He was also worshipped by the Romans.
5. **lustration**: purification by sacrifice.
6. **Mercury**: the messenger of the gods and the Roman god of merchants and trade.
7. **Flora**: see page 37.

The Best Kind of Farm

Cato the Elder, in his influential and famous book about farming, said that the best kind of farm produced a variety of things.

If you ask me what the best sort of farm is, I'll say a farm of about 1000 iugera[8] with various kinds of cultivated field in the best kind of situation. The vineyard is first in importance – provided it produces plenty of good wine. Second in value is an irrigated garden. After that, and in order of importance, willow plantation, an olive orchard, meadow-land, wheatfields, forest trees for foliage and cover, vines trained on trees, and finally an acorn wood [for pigs].

Cato the Elder, c. 160BC

8. **iugera**: units of area. 1 iugerum = 1 acre = 28,800 square feet (approx. 9600 m²)

Martial gave us a picture of his ideal small farm.

Greedy pigs follow the apron of the bailiff's wife, and the tender lamb waits for its mother's full udder. Infant slaves, born in the house, sit round the bright fire in the hearth, and thickly piled billets of wood for the fire gleam before the household gods on holidays.

Martial, c. AD86

The agricultural writer Varro reminded his readers of the commerical opportunities near a big city. The fact that olives and flowers produced more profit for the farmer meant that sometimes there was not enough grain grown for bread.

It is profitable near a city to have gardens on a large scale; for instance, of violets and roses and other products for which there is a demand in the city.

Varro, c. 80BC

Running a Farm

Books of instruction and advice were written for farmers. Cato the Elder's book is the earliest Latin book to survive complete. He and Varro gave very detailed advice about everything to do with farming, from keeping slaves content and productive, to seeds and planting, olive cultivation, presses and tools. In his book, Cato instructed the farm-manager how to treat his wife, the 'vilica'.

Make sure that the vilica carries out her duties. If the master has given her to you as your wife be satisfied with her. Make sure that she fears you. Do not let her be too extravagant. She should have as little as possible to do with the neighbours or other women, and never invite them into the house with her. She must not accept invitations to meals or go out all the time. She must be clean. She must see that the hearth is swept and tidy every night before going to bed. On feast-days she must put up a garland over the hearth. She must have food cooked for you and the other slaves. She should keep plenty of hens for eggs. She should keep dried pears, berries, figs, raisins, stewed berries and pears, grapes and quinces in jars, grape and grape-pulp in underground containers; also Praenetan nuts in underground containers. Every year she must store jars of Scantian apples and other berries. She must know how to grind flour.

Cato, c. 160BC

According to Cato, running a farm was a complicated operation. One decent-sized olive orchard needed lots of equipment.

This is how an olive orchard of two hundred and forty iugera[1] should be equipped. It should have a foreman, a foreman's wife, five labourers, three ox-drivers, one ass-driver, one swineherd, one shepherd – thirteen people altogether. There should be three teams of oxen, three asses equipped with pack-saddles to carry out the manure, one ass for mill work, and one hundred sheep. There should be five

1. iugera: see page 43.

oil-presses fully equipped including the pulping mills, a bronze cauldron to hold thirty amphorae[2], a cover for the cauldron, three iron hooks, three water pitchers, two funnels, a bronze cauldron to hold five amphorae, a cover for it, three hooks, a small vat for water, two amphorae for oil, one half-amphora, three skimming ladles, one well bucket, one wash basin, one small tray, one chamber pot, one watering pot, one ladle, one lamp stand, one sextarius measure[3]. Eight mattresses, eight spreads, sixteen pillows, ten coverlets, three towels, six cloaks made of patchwork for the slaves...

Cato, c. 160BC

Tacitus described Britain's agricultural land in his biography of his father-in-law, Agricola.

The soil is fertile and is suitable for all crops except the vine, olive and other plants requiring warmer climates. Crops grow quickly but ripen slowly. This is due to the high rainfall and dampness of the soil.

Tacitus c. AD97-98

Shortages

Food, especially bread, was often scarce in Roman times. During one food shortage the mood of the people of Rome turned ugly; in consequence, Emperor Claudius had a nasty scare, described here by Suetonius.

4. Forum: see page 30.

Claudius always gave very careful attention to looking after the city and making sure there was enough grain. When there was a grain shortage because of the prolonged drought, he was stopped in the middle of the Forum[4] by a mob of people who shouted abuse and pelted him with bits of bread. He just managed to escape and get into the palace by a back entrance. After this experience he resorted to all kinds of schemes to make sure Rome never ran short of grain, even in mid-winter. He guaranteed importers of grain the value of any wheat they might lose in storms at sea.

Suetonius, c. AD100

Religion and the Gods

Although we have evidence of magnificent Roman temples and smaller shrines, religion was more of an everyday private affair for many Romans. The temples and shrines were visited on festivals, or to make a particular request of a god, but daily offerings were made to the household shrine to keep the Lares[1], the spirits of the house, happy.

The official Roman gods were often Greek ones with new names but as the empire spread, pieces of other beliefs were absorbed from the religions of other countries. Along with the gods, many Romans placed a lot of faith in superstition, prophets, omens[2], magic and astrology. At times, the emperors themselves were worshipped as living gods.

During the Roman period, the Christian religion grew in strength. Jesus lived at this time and although Christians were initially killed for refusing to give up their faith, eventually the empire itself became Christian. The old gods were no longer worshipped and many of the superstitions were abandoned.

1. **Lares**: plural of Lar, see page 30.
2. **omens**: see page 14.

The Roman State and Religion

A Greek visitor to Rome in the 2nd century BC, the politician Polybius, believed that the pomp and ceremony of Roman religion helped unify the Roman state.

The quality in which the Roman state shows a very clear superiority is, in my view, the kind of religious conviction they have. I believe that what keeps the Roman state unified is superstition – the very thing which amongst other peoples is an object of reproach. Religious matters are wrapped in such ceremony and introduced so much into the Romans' public and private life that they could not be more present there... My own opinion is that the Romans have taken this course because of the common people... Since every great crowd is wayward, full of lawless desires, mindless passions and violent anger, it has to be controlled by unseen terrors and the display and ceremonial that goes with all that.

Polybius, c. 170BC

Temples

Public worship at temples, large and small, took place on certain festival days. Pliny the Younger thought he should rebuild a temple on his estate for these occasions.

The soothsayers[3] tell me I must rebuild the temple of Ceres[4] which stands on my property; it needs enlarging and improving, for it is certainly very old and too small considering how crowded it is on its special anniversary, when great crowds gather there from the whole district on 13 September… But there is no shelter near by from rain or sun, so I do think it would be an act of generosity and piety to build as fine a temple as I can and add porticoes[5] for the public… So will you buy me four marble columns, and marble for improving the floor and walls? We shall also have to have a new statue of the goddess, for several pieces are broken off the original wooden one… As for the porticoes … they cannot be built round the temple, for the site has a river with steep banks on one side and a road on the other. On the far side of the road is a meadow where they might be built facing the temple – unless you can think of a better solution.

Pliny the Younger, c. AD110

3. soothsayer: a person who fortells the future. In the Roman era, they were usually priests.
4. Ceres: see page 42.
5. porticoes: covered walk-ways.

Ceremonies for the Gods

The poet Virgil wrote about life in the country, and about the right way to perform a ceremony to Ceres, goddess of agriculture. Prayers, like all religious rituals, had to be correctly performed, or else the gods would be displeased.

Mix the wine with milk and honey, lead the sacrifice of your new-grown crops, while your workers follow you singing and calling the goddess Ceres to come to their homes. No-one must start cutting the wheat without first putting a wreath of oak-leaves on his head, or performing an impromptu dance in honour of Ceres, and making up verses in honour of her generosity.

Virgil, c. 40BC

STALES

VBLICA

TVIT

The Romans thought of workplaces – and houses – as having their own spirit, or *genius loci*: spirit of place. This message on an inscribed stone from Malton in Yorkshire wished the young craftsman success.

Good luck to the genius loci! Use this goldsmith's shop with as much good fortune as you can, young slave!

Inscription, 2nd or 3rd century AD

For Cicero, home and family life were sacred.

Is there anything more sacred than the home of each citizen? There he has his altars, his fireside and hearth, and his household gods. It is in his home that he performs his religious rituals and ceremonies. A citizen's house is a holy sanctuary.

Cicero, c. 45BC

At Lydney in Gloucestershire, an inscription on a curse tablet appeals for help to Nodens – who seems to be a god of healing. This Celtic god, Nodens, had been absorbed into the Roman religion in Britain.

Amongst men with the name Senicianus, keep the one who stole my ring in poor health until he returns it to the temple of Nodens.

Inscription, 4th century AD

These words are an extract from a long curse which was inscribed on a thin lead plate found in Rome. Such an 'enchantment tablet' – meant to bring evil on someone by magic – might be prepared by a professional sorcerer.

O wife of Pluto[1], good and beautiful Proserpina[2], I pray you to take away from Plotius his health and complexion, his bodily strength and his faculties... Give him the fever that comes back every third day, and the one that comes back on the fourth day, and the everyday fever too. Send someone who will bring the three-headed dog Cerberus[3] to tear out his heart... Blast him, damn him, blast him! Blast him totally!

Lead curse, c. 75-40BC

1. **Pluto**: Roman God of the Underworld.
2. **Proserpina**: as well as Pluto's wife, she was also the daughter of Ceres. Better known by her Greek name, Persephone.
3. **Cerberus**: the three-headed guard dog of the Underworld.

A papyrus from Egypt recorded the questions people often ask an 'oracle' – a priest or priestess with powers to read the future.

Am I to be sold?
Shall I be able to make it up with my children?
Am I going to get leave?
Shall I get the money?
Shall I be able to carry out my plans?
Am I going to become a beggar?
Shall I become a runaway?
Shall I become an ambassador?
Am I going to be divorced?
Have I been poisoned?

Papyrus, c. AD300

Roman officials set up many stone monuments in Britain. Some were dedications to the gods. An altar at Chesterholm, on Hadrian's Wall, had a dedication to Vulcan, god of fire.
In thanks for our temple and for the gods of the emperors, we villagers of Vindolanda set up this sacred altar to the god Vulcan[4], in willing fulfilment of the vow.

Inscription, 2nd or 3rd century AD

This altar inscription from London reflected the fact that emperors were believed to be divine.
In honour of the divine [ie imperial] house, Marcus Martiannius Pulcher, deputy imperial propraetorian legate[5] of two emperors ordered the Temple of Isis[6] ... which had fallen down through old age, to be restored.

Altar inscription, 3rd century AD

4. Vulcan: Roman god of fire and smiths.
5. deputy imperial propraetorian legate: a provincial adminstrator and judge.
6. Isis: originally an Egyptian goddess, adopted by the Romans. She was thought to protect mothers and children.

Religion and the Gods

Christians

In about AD30 a young Jewish teacher, Jesus, was executed in Jerusalem. His direct personal and one-god religion seemed to the Romans to threaten the official gods and the strength of the state. After Jesus' death, the Christian message, now banned, spread like fire. Eighty years later, Pliny the Younger, governing in Bithynia[1], had difficulty knowing what to do with Christians.

1. **Bithynia**: see page 16.

This is the line I have taken with all persons brought before me on the charge of being Christian. I have asked them in person if they are Christians, and if they admit it, I repeat the question a second and third time. If they persist, I order them to be led away to execution; for whatever the nature of their admission, I am convinced their stubbornness and obstinacy ought not to go unpunished.

Pliny the Younger, c. AD110

Saint Augustine was born in Carthage and became a Christian, a bishop, and a writer who defended the Christian religion – especially against charges that it undermined the Roman Empire. Here he ridiculed the need for so many gods.

2. **Proserpina**: see page 48.
3. **Flora**: see page 37.

Do you think the Romans dared to put their trust in a god, one god? No! As well as having Rusina to look after the countryside, they have Collina to see to the hills, while Vallonia takes care of the valleys. The goddess Segetia looks after the grain but not by herself; while it's in the ground Seia cares for it... Proserpina[2] is goddess of the first shoots of wheat, but Nodinus is god of the shoots when they grow 'knotty'. Next they have Volutrina to protect the growing blades, and Patella to protect the ears of wheat when they start to form... Then Flora[3] is their goddess for the crop flowering, Lacturtia for the whitening flower, Matuca for the crop when it is being cut, and Runcina when it has been

cut... They even need three gods for the entrance to their houses: Forculus for the door, Cardea for the hinges, and Limentuis for the threshold.

Saint Augustine of Hippo, c. AD400

4. **omen**: see page 14.
5. **Gaul**: see page 17.

Signs and Beliefs

Romans were superstitious; they believed in signs. These events of 218BC, when the Carthaginian general Hannibal had already invaded Italy, seemed like a clear forecast of disaster. Livy described the bad omens[4].

In Rome a sixth-month-old baby shouted "Victory!" in the vegetable market. In the cattle market a cow climbed up three flights of stairs then jumped out of a window. Ghost ships were seen floating across the sky... In Amiternum, ghostly men in shining garb appeared, though they did not approach anyone. In Picenum it rained stones. At Caere the writing tablets on which oracles write their responses suddenly shrank. In Gaul[5] a wolf stole a sentry's sword and ran off with it in its mouth.

Livy, late 1st century BC

Many of these popular Roman sayings might sound familiar today.

While there's life, there's hope.	Terence
Love conquers everything.	Virgil
Not worth his salt.	Petronius
No sooner said than done.	Quintus Ennius
Head over heels.	Catullus
More brawn than brain.	Cornelius Nepos

Health and Medicine

At Silchester in Britain, Roman scalpels, forceps and other medical instruments have been found. Some Roman doctors knew how to set broken bones and there were hospitals attached to certain towns and forts, such as at Hadrian's Wall in Roman Britain. Knowledge was limited to a small number of doctors, however, and there was little understanding of the internal workings of the body, or of the spread of disease.

For all this, especially in the early days, Roman medicine was mainly to do with remedies, many of which were mixed up with religion and superstition. Romans visited temples of the Greek healing gods, Apollo[1] and Aesculapius[2], asking for their help with illness.

Roman writers stressed the value of exercise and a healthy diet. But the Romans believed most passionately in lots of clean water for baths[3], and healthy sites for towns. Their engineers and architects probably contributed more to health than medicine did.

1. **Apollo**: see page 42.
2. **Aesculapius**: the god of medicine. In some myths, he was said to be the son of Apollo.
3. **baths**: see page 5.

Doctors

Many writers despised doctors, Pliny the Elder amongst them.

There is no doubt that all these [physicians], in their hunt for popularity by means of some novelty, did not hesitate to buy it with our lives. Hence those wretched, quarrelsome consultations at the bedside of the patient, no consultant agreeing with another lest he should appear to acknowledge a superior. Hence too that gloomy inscription on monuments: "It was the crowd of physicians that killed me."

Pliny the Elder, c. AD50

Plutarch expressed his view of typical Roman attitudes to doctors.

The superstitious man won't have a doctor in his house. For him, every illness or disease is sent by a god or is the result of an attack by an evil spirit.

Plutarch, c. AD100

People prefer doctors they can't understand, wrote Pliny the Elder.

Very few Roman citizens practise medicine, though it is a very profitable profession. Those who have become doctors have often simply taken up Greek medical practices. In fact no-one seems to have authority as a medical writer or doctor unless he does his research and writing in Greek – even in the eyes of those with no knowledge of Greek. Where their health is concerned, people have less faith if they understand what is written.

Pliny the Elder, c. AD50

The writer Rufus sounded more like our idea of a doctor.

You have to ask the patient questions, so that certain aspects of the illness can be understood, and the treatment made more effective. I put this matter of interrogating the patient first, since by asking questions you can find out how healthy or not his mind is. And you can get an idea of the disease itself and the part affected.

Rufus, c. AD190

A code of practice for doctors had been laid down in the *Hippocratic Corpus*, a collection of medical writings from the 5th and 4th centuries BC. It recommended that a doctor should:

... look healthy, and as plump as nature intended him to be; for the common crowd consider those who are not of this excellent bodily condition to be unable to take care of others. Then he must be clean in person, well-dressed, and anointed with sweet-smelling unguents...

Hippocratic Corpus, 4th or 5th century BC

And the Hippocratic Oath stated:

Into whatsoever houses I enter, I will enter to help the sick, and I will abstain from all intentional wrong-doing and harm, especially from abusing the bodies of man or woman, slave or free.

Hippocratic Oath, 4th century BC

Public Health

The architect Vitruvius stressed the need for towns and farms to be built in healthy places.

First in importance is a healthy site for a town. It needs to be high up, and not liable to mists or frosts. The climate shouldn't be hot or cold, just even and temperate. There shouldn't be any marshes nearby. It is bad for health if early morning breezes carry mists towards the town, laden with the poisonous breath of marsh creatures… Be very careful choosing which springs to take water from… Before deciding on a spring, check the physique of people living nearby. See if their bodies are strong and their limbs sound. Make sure they have good complexions and clear eyes.

Vitruvius, c. AD1-10

Vitruvius advised on the use of earthenware (clay), rather than lead pipes. While he had made the link between lead water pipes and ill-health, the same link wasn't made with face make-up which continued to use lead as its base.

Water supply by earthenware pipes has advantages. First, in construction: if a break occurs, anybody can repair it. Second, water is much more healthy and wholesome from earthenware pipes than from lead pipes. It seems that water can be contaminated by the lead and cause damage to health; white lead is produced, which is alleged to be harmful to the human body. For instance, workers in lead develop very pale complexions. When lead is smelted, fumes settle on the parts of the body and burn them, robbing the limbs of the strength of the blood... And the flavour from earthenware pipes is better. Everybody – even people who load their tables with silver vessels – uses earthenware to keep the water pure.

Vitruvius, c. AD1-10

Remedies and Cures

Medicine, religion and magic were closely related in Roman times. Cato the Elder's advice on how to mend bone fractures called on magic more than medical knowledge.

If any joint is dislocated it will be made well by this incantation. Take a green reed four or five feet long, snap it in half and let two men hold the halves at their hips. Begin to sing this charm – motas vaeta daries dardares astataries dissunapiter – until the halves come together, holding a sword over them all the time. When the two halves of the reed have come together, place them on the fracture and tie them there; the fracture will then be cured. Afterwards, say the incantation daily over the fracture. This alternative form can be used – haut aut haut tarsis ardannabou dannaustra.

Cato the Elder, c. 160BC

Pliny the Elder, in his *Natural History*, mentioned some other interesting Roman remedies

If a horse casts a shoe, and someone retrieves it, it will cure an attack of hiccoughs.

A remedy for patients with depression is calf's dung boiled in wine.

People suffering from lethargy and loss of energy can be roused to action by first steeping in vinegar the calluses from the legs of an ass, and then applying them to the nostrils. The same result comes from bringing to the nose the strong fumes of goats' horns or of their hair, or wild boar's liver.

Pliny the Elder, c. AD50

Travelling eye-doctors carried their own sticks of ointment which they stamped with their name and what the ointment was for.

Gaius Valerius Amandus's vinegar salve for running eyes.
Gaius Valerius Amandus's drops for dim sight.
Gaius Valerius Valentinus's mixture for clear sight.

Eye-doctors' stamps, 1st or 2nd century AD

Diet and Lifestyles

In the first century AD, a great survey was made by the writer Celsus of the science of medicine as the Romans understood it. It was still being read 1,500 years later.

Anyone who has worked all day ... should set aside some part of it to look after the body. His priority should be exercise, which he should do before eating. The more the work has involved the mind rather than the body, the more exercise he should do. But exercise should be light for those whose work is more physical than mental.

Celsus, c. AD40

The importance of diet was stressed by Galen, who became a kind of imperial court doctor. His many books included one called *Staying Healthy*, which had recipes like this – still useable – for health-giving foods and drinks.

Oxymeli – honey vinegar. Simmer the honey till it foams, then skim off the scum and discard it. Add enough vinegar so it's not too sharp or too sweet. Boil it again, reducing it till it's properly blended... To drink, mix it with water, just as you mix wine with water.

Galen, c. AD150

Games and Pastimes

1. **amphitheatres**: see page 5.
2. **baths**: see page 5.
3. **quinquennial**: a fifth anniversary celebration.

Roman people liked to enjoy themselves, both publicly in the specially-built theatres and amphitheatres[1], and privately at home. We know of toys for the children, board games similar to backgammon and literary readings. Socializing was a great pleasure, whether at the public baths[2] or dining out at a friends' home.

The Romans built huge arenas, some of which survive today, to watch plays, chariot-racing, gladiatorial contests and extraordinarily spectacular shows. Writers tell us of public shows provided by emperors to keep the mass of the people happy. One day in two was a holiday with free entertainment. Many Romans of later times grew to despise the blood-soaked contests.

Gladiatorial Games

Gladiators were slaves, trained to fight to the death for the entertainment of others. The shows were advertised. This was found scrawled on a wall in Pompeii.

Thirty pairs of gladiators provided by Gnacus Alleius Nigidius Maius ... together with their replacements, will fight at Pompeii on November 24, 25, 26. There will be a hunt. Hurrah for Maius the quinquennial[3]!

Graffiti, Pompeii, before AD79

This lucky charm, found at York, belonged to a gladiator or a charioteer.

Sir Victor, may you be victorious and lucky.

Bone charm, 3rd or 4th century AD

Seneca was one of those who found gladiatorial combats disgusting. This particular kind of fight was timed for mid-day, the time he 'dropped in'; the fighters were not trained gladiators, and had no real defensive armour.

I happened to drop in at the lunch-time show, expecting to see some comic turns, a little light relief from the spectacle of human blood. Quite the contrary. The previous combats were merciful in comparison. Now they got down to business. It was pure, unadulterated murder. The men have no way to protect themselves. They leave their bodies wide open, and every blow tells. There's no helmet or shield to interfere with the swordplay. Who needs armour? Who needs skill? Such things only postpone the moment of death. In the morning they throw men to the lions and bears, at noon they throw them to the crowd. Kill, then be killed, that's the rule. Win one bout, be slaughtered in the next.

Seneca, c. AD30

Some emperors – Caligula, Hadrian, Lucius Verus – tried their hand at gladiatorial combat as amateurs. Commodus, before he was strangled in AD192, had as many as a thousand bouts in the arena as a professional gladiator. He had particular fun slaughtering animals. Herodian, born in AD180 and so a possible eye-witness, was impressed.

Everybody was amazed by his [Commodus's] shooting. Using arrows with curved tips, he shot at Moroccan ostriches, running as fast as their legs and flapping wings could carry them and, the tops of their necks severed by the force of the blow, they went on running, though decapitated, as if nothing had happened. A leopard charged and got its teeth into the hunter who challenged it, and was on the point of mauling him when Commodus at the vital moment struck it with his spear, killing it and saving its victim. A hundred lions were released from below ground. With a hundred shots he killed them all; there they lay, all over the arena, and people had plenty of time to count them and see that not a single shot had missed its mark.

Herodian, c. AD200

58

Even emperors who were not naturally cruel seemed to feel the need to put on 'games' to keep the people happy. Suetonius described Claudius' entertainments.

Claudius built warships and manned them with 19,000 fighters, surrounding the ships with a ring of rafts to prevent escape. In the middle there was plenty of space for ships to be manoeuvred by hard rowing, and skilful steering, and to perform straight-forward ramming – everything as in a real sea-battle... The shore of the lake and the slopes and hillside above, just like a stadium, were packed with spectators from the neighbouring towns and from Rome itself... Claudius presided in a splendid military cloak, with Agrippina his wife in a cloak made of cloth of gold. Though the fighters were criminals, they fought bravely. A great deal of blood was shed, but they were spared total extermination.

Suetonius, c. AD100

Suetonius, born in AD70 might have seen the show put on by Domitian (emperor AD81-96).

Domitian put on gladiatorial shows at night, by torchlight, in which women fought as well as men.

Suetonius, c. AD100

Romans loved these sickening murderous entertainments. Suetonius pictured the scene on the road to the arena.

So many people thronged to these shows that visitors often pitched tents along the roads, and the crush was so great sometimes that many people died.

Suetonius, c. AD100

XXXII

Literary Readings

Romans did have many other pleasures which were less barbaric. Interestingly, literary readings – public recitals of poems, stories and other writing – were extremely popular. Suetonius described the scholarly Claudius' first reading.

While he was still a boy Claudius [the Emperor-to-be] started work on a Roman history... When he gave his first public reading to a packed audience he found it difficult to hold their attention because at the very beginning of his performance an extremely fat man came in, sat down on a bench, which collapsed under him, sending several of his neighbours sprawling, and creating great amusement. Even when silence had been restored the young Claudius could not help recalling the sight and going off into peels of laughter.

Suetonius, c. AD100

Readings could also be boring, as experienced by Seneca.
He brings an enormous work of history, in very small writing, tightly folded together. He reads a large part of it, then says, "I'll stop now, if you like." Immediately there's a shout of, "Carry on! Carry on!" from people who'd like him to be struck dumb on the spot.

Seneca, c. AD30

Dining with Friends

One of life's great pleasures for Roman men was the dining party, an evening spent eating and drinking in the company of friends – and perhaps musicians and dancing girls. Pliny the Younger, in a letter to a friend, Septius Clarus, complained about him not coming to dinner, and preferring less interesting food and company.

You accepted my invitation to dinner and then didn't come! Your punishment will have to be to pay all my expenses, the full cost of it. It was nicely laid out, one lettuce each, three snails, two eggs, barley-cake, wine with honey chilled with snow (an expensive dish, because the snow disappears in the dish), as well as olives, beetroots, gherkins, onions, and any number of other delicacies. You would have heard a comic play, a reader, a singer – all three if you felt generous. Instead you went where you could have oysters, sow-innards, sea-urchins, and Spanish dancing girls. You will suffer for this – I won't say how. It was a cruel trick.

Pliny the Younger, c. AD100

This Roman 'inn-sign' – actually a stone inscription addressed to hunters – has some neat alliteration.
Abemus in cena – pullum piscem pernum paonem – venatores

Translation:
We have in the kitchen – chicken fish ham peacock – huntsmen
Inscription, date unkown

The Public Baths

The public baths were popular meeting spots as well as a place to wash. Seneca wrote this sketch of activity at the baths, after he had made the mistake of renting rooms above them.

My lodgings are right over the public baths. Imagine all the different noises I have to listen to... When the muscle-man is exercising with the barbells, either working hard or putting on a good act, I can hear every grunt, and the wheezing and panting when he lets his breath out. Then there's the idler who drops in for a cheap massage. I can't just hear the slap of the masseur's hand on his shoulders, I can even tell whether the hand's cupped or flat! And then there's the resident pro shouting scores, and as well as all this, there's normally a drunk or pickpocket being hauled off by the police. Not to forget the man who has to sing in the bath, the bathers who like to hit the water with a huge splash, the shouts of "cakes for sale", "hot sausages", "get your sweets here"!

Seneca, c. AD30

Timeline

BC

753 Legendary founding of Rome.

c. 600 Earliest Latin inscriptions.

c. 616-509 Rome ruled by Etruscan kings.

493 Latin league formed with neighbours for mutual defence.

449 The Twelve Tables, a code of law, are publicized.

396 Rome takes over new territory.

340-338 Rome defeats the Latin league.

312 Rome's first aqueduct.

c. 280 First Roman coins issued.

275 Rome rules southern Italy.

264 Earliest record of gladiatorial combat.

264-241 War with Carthage, Rome wins. Sicily becomes a Roman province.

218-201 Second war with Carthage, Hannibal invades but Rome
wins again.

197 Rome defeats Philip V of Macedon in Greece.

160 Cato writes book on agriculture.

146 Cathage destroyed. North Africa becomes a Roman province, as does Greece.

133-129 Rome gains control of the province of Asia (part of modern Turkey).

121 Rome conquers southern Gaul.

81 Sulla becomes dictator.

73-71 Spartacus leads slave revolt.

58-51 Julius Caesar campaigning in Gaul, acquiring northern Gaul for Rome.

54-55 Caesar in Britain.

49-48 Civil wars in Rome.

46 Caesar appointed dictator for 10 years.

44 Caesar assassinated.

43 Cicero dies.

c. 35-30 Horace's *Satires* appear.

c. 33-16 Poet Propertius composing *Elegies*.

30 Egypt taken over.

28 Roman temples restored.

27 Octavian becomes emperor with name Augustus. Spain becomes a province of Rome.

AD

14 Death of Augustus. He is declared a god of Rome by the Senate.
Tiberius becomes emperor.

19 Death of Virgil, *Aenaed* published.

30 Jesus Christ is crucified.

37 Caligula becomes emperor.

41 Claudius becomes emperor.

43 Conquest of Britain begins.

54 Nero becomes emperor. Rules until 68.

60-61 Revolt of the Iceni in Britain under Boudica.

64 Rome burnt, Nero persecutes Christians.

77 Pliny the Elder's *Natural History* is published (in 102 volumes).

78-84 Agricola govenor of Britain.

79 Vesuvius erupts, destroying Pompeii – Pliny the Elder dies investigating it.

84 Agricola conquers lowlands of Scotland.

86 First of the poet Martial's *Epigrams* are published.

97 Trajan becomes emperor.

100 The first of Juvenal's *Satires* are published.

112 Pliny the Younger dies.

114 Trajan builds a great column in Rome to celebrate his victories in war.

117 Hadrian emperor until 138.

118-120 Hadrian rebuilds Pantheon in Rome.

120 Historian Tacitus dies.

132-5 Hadrian builds his Wall in northern England.

212 Roman citizenship granted to all free citizens of the Roman Empire.

252 Roman provinces in Europe attacked by Goths and others.

303 Strong persecution of Christians under Diocletian.

306 Constantine is made Emperor while on a visit to York.

313 Constantine grants toleration to Christians.

330 Constantine makes Constantinople new capital of the empire.

395 Empire divided into Eastern and Western halves.

400 Hadrian's Wall abandoned.

410 Rome pulls out of Britain.

430 Roman money goes out of use in Britain.

450 Saxons begin to settle in Britain.

455 Vandals burn Rome.

476 Germanic chieftain Odoacer deposes last western emperor of Rome.

1453 Conquest of Constantinople by Turks and the final end of Eastern Roman (or Byzantine) Empire.

Index

MAXIMO